1979

Signature New and Selected Poems

Signature

New and Selected Poems

Bonaro W. Overstreet

W · W · Norton & Company · Inc · New York

Library of Congress Cataloging in Publication Data

Overstreet, Bonaro Wilkinson, 1902–
  Signature.

  Includes indexes.
          I. Title.
PS3529.V37S5   811'.5'2   77–25117
  ISBN 0-393-04504-8
  ISBN 0-393-04511-0 pbk.

In Memory of H.A.O.

Contents

Acknowledgment

Many of the poems in this book have previously appeared in newspapers and magazines, as well as in earlier books of my poems, FOOTSTEPS ON THE EARTH, which is now out of print, and HANDS LAID UPON THE WIND, published by Norton. I wish to say thanks to the publisher of the former book, Alfred A. Knopf, and to *The Saturday Evening Post, The Ladies' Home Journal, The New York Sun, The National Parent-Teacher, PM, Progressive Education, Better Homes and Gardens, Voices, Bozart, New Democracy,* and *Poetic Viewpoint.*

Signature New and Selected Poems

In spite of heat and hardpan; or the silence
Of her who will not let them die if care
Can keep them blooming to the summer's end.

There may be delicate different ways of saying
That life is good to live. But this will do.

Stubborn Ounces

*(To One Who Doubts the Worth of Doing
Anything if You Can't Do Everything)*

You say the little efforts that I make
will do no good: they never will prevail
to tip the hovering scale
where Justice hangs in balance.
                                    I don't think
I ever thought they would.
But I am prejudiced beyond debate
in favor of my right to choose which side
shall feel the stubborn ounces of my weight.

Introduction to Philosophy

Young spruces stood bolt upright, every twig
Stiff with refusal to be beat by snow.
Young hemlocks sloped their boughs beneath the load,
Letting it softly go.

Each solved, no doubt, to its own satisfaction
The problem posed by uninvited weight.
I'd not take sides with either. I have tried
Both ways of handling fate.

Long Ago

Father shortened his pace and I stretched mine—
Which made for our going together along a trail
That followed a ridge to the sky. Where it went we went,
With spring as a reason for going, and the wind upon us.

Not to the sky did we come: the sky strode off
Faster than we were striding: we topped the crest
And saw how the sky had put hill upon colored hill
Between its going and our own. But we did not care.

That was a day that was not like any other:
The round sun overhead, grown ancient with seasons,
Did not remark that father was older than I:
And the little grass, spongy with emerald newness,
Did not label me young. We were two who tramped
Equally side by side and lifted our voices
To call as meadowlarks call, each note a blossom
Briefly opened in air and golden-petaled.
Kind to our feet was the intricate blossoming earth.
We drank from streams that were chill to our cupped hands,
Clean and chill to our mouths. . . .

                              The ancient sun
Grew older down in the west. The shadows of trees
Were written long and longer across green hollows.

Father shortened his pace and I stretched mine
As we followed the homeward trail. Hills stood behind.
Roofs were ahead, and farmhouse smoke climbed to the cool
                    of the evening.

Elegy for a Country Store

Now that the store has been taken by clean fire,
Red in the night, a sudden banner on darkness,
A crackle more sharp than the slow noise of the years
That have lain in dust on the shelves, that have rubbed the
  counters
Elbow-smooth, and have hollowed the splintery boards of the
  floor . . .
Now that the store is gone, I will bring remembrance
Like sun warm upon charred beams or wind fingering the ashes.

Now that the store is gone, it is old no longer—
No longer shabby with scaled paint, no longer cobwebbed in
  corners.
It has become again the store I knew in my childhood.

The after-harvest clink of metal that nourished a till
Grown gaunt through long months of flimsy feeding on credit
Might ring like coin to the ear.
                    But the hands and the eyes of farmers
Knew it for more than coin: in its hardness the juice of the grape
Ran scarlet runnels as surely as juice trickled down the hubs
Of the overloaded wagons that creaked on the winery road.
The purple of prunes, the amber of sun-cured hay,
The gold of peaches, the acrid odor of walnuts,
And the long smell of the earth: these slid into the till:
And the till was fed.
                    And farmers' wives
Came to shop for Thanksgiving.
And the children of farmers came.
                    I was one of the children.
I know how it was to feel the two-way tug of desire
When the glass door shut behind me and I was safe inside:

On my right, the cases of candy, the nuts, the fat store
    cheeses . . .
On my left, the laces and ribbons, color climbing on color,
The stacked-up bolts of ginghams, worsteds, challies, serges . . .
I know how it was to sit on top of a creaking stool,
With mother beside me, to choose cloth for a winter school dress:
The dress that had been postponed till harvest was cash in the
    hand.
Nothing like that in the world: nothing ever so lovely
As the lifting down from the shelves of the stripes, the plaids, the
    plain colors;
The rhythmic thump on the counter of the over-and-over-turning
Plump bolt as the clerk measured the chosen yardage.

Nothing so lovely . . . save times when I trailed my father
Into the hardware room of the pungent leathery odors,
Of subtle plowshare gleams and the frank shining of washtubs,
Of dishes dusty on shelves but willing enough to yield
To my furtively rubbing finger their secrets of flower and
    gold . . .

Christmas came to the store—and we came with it,
Under loopings of tinsel, under wax-candle light.
And delicate Spring that hovered in fragrant bloom on the
    orchards
Came to the shelves of the store in dimity, cross-bar muslin,
Organdie sprigged with pink, polka-dot prints.
Spring came into the store—and we came with it.

The Fourth of July came, snapping with firecrackers,
Spluttery with Roman candles, dizzy with pinwheels . . .

But the store is gone now, in red fire running
Swift on the track of the years that had left it behind.

First Day of Teaching

Now this is new: that I (habitué
Of classes where my thinking has been stirred
To surging tide or frothy ripple) stand
Before a class to speak instructive word.
I planned to have it so. Deliberately
I laid foundation for this moment. Yet . . .
I did not know my feet would feel so large . . .
O God of Teachers, may I not forget
Those neat assignments, practiced to the letter,
Those deftly fashioned phrases that I planned.
Now must I pass these papers. O dear God,
Let not the sheets go slithering from my hand.
And if You could but ring the fire alarm . . .
Or anything . . . O any sharp surprise
To turn away from my stiff dwindling self
These thirty pair of adolescent eyes.

Oil Town

Under the sun,
Criss-crossing row on row,
The streets flow north and south,
And east and west they flow;
And every one
Ends as it was begun—
Level upon the tawny level plain;
And over all, the baying hungry mouth
Of brazen sky.
The thirsty sod perspires in goldenrod.
Torpid and limp the conquered prairies lie;
While spectre-framed the vampire derricks stand,
Sucking the sluggish dark blood of the land.

Portrait of a Young Scientist

His curiosity would peel the stars—
Would pick their prickles off, would split the rind.
And if he found an inner pulp of darkness,
That too would tease the fingers of his mind.
He loves this world—in pieces.
                            Bit by bit,
He turns it over in his wondering hands—
Too diffident to deal in absolutes,
And still amazed at what he understands.

Conversion

Now am I credulous
Of all old ghosts:

Have I not met
The prairie-walking wind?

Have I not seen the tumbleweeds go by
Under the moon?

Chant After Drought

Mighty the Sower who tramples the cloud-lands,
Flinging abroad his curved handfuls of rain-seed.
Mightily echo among the ribbed mountains
The songs of his planting.

Seeds that are quick with a stranger intention
Than any that fly from the hand of a mortal
Fall to the earth with a silvery patter—
Fall, and are hidden

Under a soil that grows dark with their magic.
Fragrant and cool with the mystery of seeding
Now lie the fields that but yesterday slumbered
Sun-choked and dusty.

Strangely, this seed that is silver will issue
Into the crystalline green of the cornstalk,
Into the silk that is soft on the corn-ear;
Into the grasslands.

Mighty the Sower who tramples the cloud-lands,
Flinging abroad his deep song and his rain-seed.
Grateful the hands of the little earth-planters
Lifted to praise him.

After a Time

I will not let it happen—not to me—
This far-too-sober teacher-tendency
To see oneself as chosen instrument
Whereby the solemn truth effects descent
From generation unto generation.
I will reject all stamp of my vocation
And be a *person*—curious, young, and free.
I will not bow to the monotony
Of checking grades.
                 And never will I act
As though a student's wholeness could be packed
Into that special fragment of his brain
Devoted to my class.
              I will retain
The right, the wish, to be a growing cell
Among my human peers.
                I now rebel . . .
Yes, now: this moment: off me I will throw
Octopus arms. Invisibly they grow
To squeeze my thought—which once ran swift and keen—
Into a stodgy pattern of routine.

I will be blithe tonight. The wind is high.
I will walk out alone beneath the sky
And let the whirling leaves spin past my feet,
And breathe a rain-damp air and know it sweet.
I will talk with one who loves the feel of laughter
Along a night-cool throat.
             And after . . . after . . .
In the enfolding quiet of my room
I will dream before a mirror in half gloom.

This I will do.
                    But first, to clear my mind
Of any care for what is left behind,
I'll just run briskly through this sheaf of papers
To see what type of curious mental capers
The students now have managed—to my sorrow.
And I will plan a bit about tomorrow . . .

Now for the wind, the night . . .

                              Perhaps, instead,
I'll call it one more day, and go to bed . . .

One Part of a Teacher's Mind

There is no thing more difficult to teach
Than simply this: that what is known to man
Is but the golden center of a blossom
Wide-petaled by his ignorance. If that center
Mature and yield its ripened store of seed,
Yet each new flower that sways upon new stem
Is vivid heart and circling petal-fringe.
And what is known to any single mortal
Is but a blowing grain of pollen dust.

What do I understand?—a modicum
About the habits of the words that wait
Upon our speaking needs; and something more
About the largeness and the littleness
Of what the generations have remarked
Concerning life they live and death they die.
These I would treat with honor: no small thing
It is when phrases stand equivalent
To body and soul caught in the ache of being.
And truths there are that I have learned by living.
Yet what I do not know so widely circles
This firm bright core that everywhere I turn
I face elusive, noncommittal worlds.

One student wears upon a slender wrist
A bracelet that she fashioned for such wearing—
And to the making of it brought a knowledge
That I do not possess. A sober boy
Who has few words to say yet laid his hands
Lovingly on material and devised
A chair that speaks the loveliness of form.
Not so my hands are wise in handling wood.
Another boy comes grimy with the oil

Of the recalcitrant machines he tames
Each afternoon—and I stare at him, sensing
How many subtle things his stubby fingers
Are deft in doing. And one slight, somber girl
Can lift the vibrant shape of violin
And waken such a lingering lonesome sob
That I—who am not intimate with strings—
Am weighted with my caring for man's caring
About his isolation and his wonder.
Again, again, again the students flock—
And each is vessel of an understanding
That is not mine.
                    And all of us together—
And all our forebears who are lost in time—
Could marshall wisdom that would be a whiff
Of golden pollen on a casual wind . . .

Yet somehow I and these, my younger peers,
Must learn our ways of wisely being unwise—
The manner that is fitting in the instance
Where duly tested knowledge is our own;
The manner that is gracious with admission
That here and there we move but as we must,
Lacking certainty, yet being alive
And bound to some behavior by that being;
The manner that is poise without defiance
Before the one who proves us ignorant;
And most of all, the standing at our ease
In the large enigma of the universe.

Not without care have I devised techniques
For showing how one word and another word
Dovetail to frame a sentence. It is good
To handle neatly things that fit together
So that their sum is meaning.
                        But I stand
Explaining this and that—and suddenly . . .
The chalk that traces curlycues, and dribbles
Pale tiny sprays of dust . . . the feel of words

That are a warmth or coolness in my mouth . . .
Some book that stands grave witness of my speaking . . .
A certain face remote with private thoughts . . .
Beyond the classroom window, splendid sun
That burnishes the leaves of cottonwoods:
All these press in around me with their forms;
And with no words, they say the life we live
Is very spacious . . .
                    Oh, I need to learn
What silent answer can be made by man
When such as these speak with their tongues of silence.

A Very Small Farm

To C. S. W.

Truly a farm that measures fifteen acres
Is frugal portion of this goodly earth.
To one whose sight is stretched by prairie-seeing,
This scanty fragment may seem fit for mirth.

Yet here is room for man to turn the furrow
That leaves dark loam to crumble in the sun;
And room to savor the deep harvest-peace
That comes to orchards with their fruitage done.

One does not need broad lands to listen well
To rhythms played by rain for waiting seeds.
Narrow vineyards can be overlaid
By warm sap-odors when the pruned branch bleeds.

And he who owns a single tree has room
To learn how black twigs quicken into bloom.

Unwitnessed

No eye beheld the colors that bannered from my hand.
No ear but mine heard bugles drip splendor on the land.
No one read the sunrise that wrote out fiery news,

Nor guessed that little feathered wings were fitted to my shoes.

Small blame to them: how could they know? how could they hear
  or see?
There was no witness when your eyes spoke love to me.

Prairie Night

Yes, it is true: if there be perfect form
It is the circle.
                    You and I, this night,
Stood center of earth-circle wide as sight,
While over us, in sky new-washed by storm,
The circle-moon dripped flawless ivory light.

Warning

Let him who buys beware:
The step at midnight on the creaking stair
Will be that of a child who once was there.
I warn: she will be there.
A board or two will creak in the attic floor . . .
Then nothing more . . .

The child I was will roam the lane at night
When moon above and blossoming trees are white:
A shadow—nothing more—against the white.
A shadow, and a petal's sudden fall . . .
That will be all . . .

This little haunting ghost will not be shy
Even of daylight and the wide blue sky:
She will skip by,
Ruffling the fallen leaves and the spent grass.
Lightly and soft as leaves fall, she will pass.

The child who once was there will still be there.
Let him who buys beware.

This Morning

This morning laid its beauty at my feet;
And I, responsively, bowed down my heart
Before that beauty.
              It is suitable
That mortal man and mortal universe
Thus render mutual praise.
                      They have their hour.
There will be time, and more than time enough,
Beyond all mornings and all human hearts,
For the immortal to remain unbowed.

Two Work Horses in a Pasture

There is this to be remembered about horses:
They have been around on this earth for a long time.
They stand solid.
The planet testifies
Their ancient grant holds good.
The faded name it bears is genuine.
The four-toed signature of Eohippus.

God Started Something ...

God started something when he made a man,
And made a woman who must smile at him
Because her love lies smiling in her heart.
Some hold he fashioned sorrow and long pain.
I say the strangest product of that hour
(And He surprised as any when He saw it)
Was earth's first trembling beautiful awareness
That two need not be two, but may be one.

Before Dawn

In the long silent hour before the dawn,
I awoke to a great peace.

In the street, one solitary bulb
Rifted the darkness, and against its light
A pepper branch was stenciled, black and keen.
Three stars were tangled in the topmost bough . . .

And because deep loveliness was there,
I thought of you . . .

Thank You

I speak with a new confidence: my words
No longer rattle in an empty space
And leave me with a foolish-feeling face
When they are gone.
                    They are as birds
That from your understanding borrow grace
To spiral skyward and to tilt clear sound
Back to the old opacity of ground.

But yours the credit: yours the subtle ear
That fashions beauty from plain words you hear.

Rain Over a New Roof

So silvery slight was the first fall of rain
We should have missed its coming but for leaves
That murmured quick surprise along the eaves
And tapped excitement on the window-pane.

But having heard, we left our fireside places
And went together into the cool night
To see the slope of rain in casement light,
To feel the slope of rain upon our faces.

Then, swiftly as it came, the shower was over.
It scampered eastward with a running breeze,
Leaving no keepsake but the drip of trees
And the damp touch of ankle-brushing clover.

The shower was gone. We lingered, you and I,
To hear the beeches say that rain is sweet . . .
To notice how the crowding clouds ran fleet . . .
To watch a quiet moon take back the sky.

Wind Across the Heavens

There was wind across the heavens,
And within our walls great peace . . .

You were reading to me.
Candles wedged the twilight of our room;
My dress glowed crimson in their light.
Words and candle flame and shimmering silk
Blended to one quiet harmony
Against the dark enchantment of life.

There was wind across the heavens,
And within our walls great peace . . .

Before Sleeping

New grass will wave in a new wind . . . tomorrow . . .
White buds will blur our orchard lanes again.
Clouds will rise for a brief flying . . . tomorrow . . .
And earth will feel the narrow feet of rain.

Streams will wash their pebbles white . . . tomorrow . . .
Each shaken fern will yield a twinkling shower.
Meadowlarks will spend their songs . . . tomorrow . . .
And sun-drenched clearings will be glad with flower.

The wide lift of blue sky . . . tomorrow . . .
Will glimmer from beyond each leafing bough.
I will walk out into the woods . . . tomorrow . . .
                              tomorrow . . .
I will sleep now . . .

Scenery

Scenery is what we look at for an hour, for a day,
But with no will to alter
What our eyes acknowledge.
If it stabs our inertia to no wonder,
If it fails to quiet us with the peace of long distances,
Ours is the privilege of withholding admiration.
Scenery is that which must bear the burden of proof
Before we need name it excellent:
We have no plans concerning it.

We who have split devotion into parts—
One for the western seaboard of this land,
One for the eastern—and have learned to take
An intervening continent for our province,
Are not unversed in scenery:
                                        we remember
How gaunt pines climb the ridges of the Rockies,
And how, where pine trees falter to dead stubs,
The white peaks climb in loneliness to jab
The invulnerable sky.
We know the chasm of the Yellowstone:
Green river whipped to white by waterfalls,
And melting back to green, and a green flowing
Between clay banks banded with blue and umber.
In the Dakota Bad Lands we have tasted
Such silence that our throats were puffed to pain
By their tight mortal need to break that silence.
And out across the Border from El Paso
We saw one mighty purple morning rise.

Scenery is what we look at for an hour, for a day,
Itself exempt from time: no moorings hold it
To past or future.

Do you remember how, one afternoon,
A sailboat skimmed the waters at La Jolla?
Never for us will those white wings be furled.
Never for us will that blue bay be chafed
By any storm.
Do you remember Colorado Canyon
Mauve and rust-red in the twilight?
Never for us will morning nibble the stars
That came above the level-rimmed horizon
While we two watched.

Scenery is majestic furniture
For human minds.
But it is not enough.

By many scenic highways have we come
To find this plot of earth that grimes our fingers
And raises on the palm of either hand
A constellation of small callouses;
That brings our walking to a sudden halt
Because persistent ragweed bustles up
To taunt us with its scrubby tufts of green . . .

And all the days that move across these acres
Go hand in hand with time.
Already we have memories to cherish:
We know where violets blossom in the Spring . . .
Hepaticas . . . and trilliums . . . and wild ginger;
We know the way the brook outclimbs the bank
After a night of storm, to cry new freedom . . .

These are things to talk of while we stroll
Among the fireflies of a summer dusk.
These, and chores we mean to do tomorrow . . .
Next week . . . next month . . . before the frost sets in . . .

Scenery has use for magnitude and grandeur.
But very modest land is good enough
For him so saturate with its wind and rain

That if he stands too long on a summer morning
With sun upon his back, he feels impelled
To step aside lest he should send down roots
And find himself with leaves instead of hair.

Residuum

Corn fields
When the yellow ears have been garnered,
When dry stalks slant and dangle stiff leaves,
Are places of wind-music.
Even so do the long winds of time
Make harmony from husks and sapless stalks
Of old creeds.

Fireflies

With what a quaint extravagance of light
The inventive universe compounded these
From fire and flight.

Yet there was something of a large compassion
In so devising for this fickle planet
Stars after its own fashion.

Spring Sewing

My wardrobe has been set aright.
For as the Spring comes round,
I must from morning until night
Go forth correctly gowned.

So here's a primrose yellow—
A proper dress for one
To wear on mornings mellow
With clean new sun.

A crimson scarf for this dull grey,
Like sorrow cut with laughter,
Or storm clouds on an April day
With sunset after.

Cool sweep of blue chiffon;
Ruffled lace as white
As almond blossoms in the dawn,
Or dim starlight . . .

It seems incredible that I
Have wrought these lovely things:
As though I shaped a butterfly,
Or curved a bluebird's wings.

But though I walk so radiantly—
Each gown a fresh surprise—
No neighbor turns to stare at me
With envy in her eyes.

Instead, in pity and distress,
They murmur, "Oh, my dear . . .
I see she's making that old dress
Last through another year!"

Extra Prayer

God, have You room up there—
Room to spare
Within the archives of man's high desires—
For one small extra prayer?
If be You have,
Then give ear while I pray
That You, this Summer day,
Most tenderly uphold in Your strong hands
The hopes of those who set up roadside stands.
Send customers their way
Who oddly seek, and willingly will pay
For pillowcases bordered with crochet.
Send customers for corn and plums and jam,
For home-made bread and home-cured country ham,
And garden flowers picked under morning skies
(So soon to wilt and fade if no one buys).
Let all who wait and hope have luck today . . .
And sleep rewarded . . .
     This, God, I do pray.

The Redeeming Risk

(*Luke 19:1–10*)

Admitting disadvantage, being small
Where crowding men stood tall,
Zacchaeus hied him up a sycamore tree
The better the Lord to see;
And from that height there was vouchsafed to him
The view allotted only to that mortal
Who climbs out on a limb.

Zacchaeus had not figured: down on earth,
His mind had never brought the thought to birth
That, balancing at a precarious height,
Man sees—but likewise puts himself in sight.
He stared at Christ, viewed clearly from that limb.
But Christ looked back at him.

Above the press of crowding, curious folk,
Eye countered eye; and it was Christ who spoke:
"Come down, Zacchaeus. I'm going home with you."
Zacchaeus scrambled down more rapidly
Than he had climbed the tree;
And what he knew, he knew.

He stood with Christ, and his words were tumbling joy:
"Listen . . . half that I own I will employ
To feed your poor. And wealth I haven't earned
Except by power and guile will be returned
Fourfold to those who suffered.
                              Is that your way?"
"You will be blessed fulfilling what you say."

If you would add a moral to the story,
Let it be this: no man afraid of glory

Should climb out on a limb—for at that height
Earth shows in new perspective and the sight
Is hard on wealth's self-made pomposity.
Let only valiant men go climb a tree.

Night Song

This is a day when we have loved and laughed
And gone befriended
By small white flowers and white clouds in the sky.
Now it is ended.

This is a day when sun has warmed our shoulders.
But the day is over.
Now comes the twilight wind along the hills:
That eerie rover

Acquainted with the moon, and the moon's path
Upon the lake,
And the thin reeds that bend with a dark singing
For the wind's sake.

Now we shall wander homeward in the dusk,
Subdued and slow,
As those who cherish well an ended day
Are wont to go.

And we shall sleep while white stars in the sky
Blossom and fade,
And while the trees beneath the moon lay down
Westward, then east, their shade.

We shall sleep well, with the compassionate dark
To smooth our dreams to quietness; and after,
We shall awake to meet another day
Of love and laughter.

Should I Bother Him?

I hesitated on this side of prayer
Lest God be concentrating on some thought
(The way you often are) that should not be
Invaded by my coming.
                              Then I prayed.
For I have learned from you how it would be:
He'd only look preoccupied a moment
Until His mind could shift and His eyes clear—
To let me know I had a right to come.

If I Live to Be an Old Woman . . .

If I live to be an old woman I will live in this house.
Memory will sleep in my bed and will rise at morning
To walk by my side through these rooms, to look at the
    mountain.
I will go slow on the stone steps carrying firewood.
My back will curve as I climb, as the backs of the old
Curve with the questions left at the end of life.
And then at morning or evening I will leave,
Never to stand again at this wide window
We loved into place because of our love of a mountain.

Feet of Clay

They warn me you have feet of clay,
O precious idol I adore.
But—strange effect—their scoffing words
Have only made me love you more.
For always when I worship you
My waiting thoughts, released, take wing—
So if the words they speak are true,
Then clay most be a lovely thing.

Lick Observatory

Not God alone decreed, "Let there be light!"
Swift the command that thundered in His tone.
But longer searching struggle with the night
Has been our own.
Holding no Word with which to open sight,
Our cries have blown
More futile than dry leaves across the height
Of dark infinity.
               Yet we have sown
Cool seeds of patience, able to requite
The faith of careful planting, and have known
This wonder of obscurity made bright.

Dusk

Dusk came down to the pond-edge . . .
Water lilies that all day long
Had swayed in the sun
Closed timorous petals and hid away
From the brooding night.

We who had sat on the grass-bank,
Watching the lilies sway in the sun,
Lay back . . . and looked for stars.

Night Whistle

When the two trains met in the darkness,
And passed on their way into darkness,
The whistle of ours was a question mark:
A thin straight lift and a silvery curve,
Like a sickle for harvesting stars.

Perspective

I shall remember
That we need not oblige the universe
To bulge,
Making room for us.
Have I not seen
Two men
On a hand-car
In Kansas?

From a Train Window

Others will know this farm in other guise:
Brittle with frost, or slushy under rain.
They will observe how softly fields grow green
With sprouting grain.

Others will be intimate: these acres
For them will be a place of slow maturing—
For yearly haps and mishaps that invoke
Rejoicing or enduring.

But I will hold one image as a charm
Against all change: the vague translucent light
That in this moment cherishes a farm
Released from night.

I shall know always how dark house and barn,
Dark quivering trees, and stiff dark shocks of corn
Lean on the breast of silence when wide sky
Is streaked with morn.

I shall know how a dark-framed wagon rests
Beside a shed; and how two horses stand
Dark on a slope where a dark fence-line runs
Across dim land.

To a Deserted House in Utah

Houses do not grow from alkali
As stiff grasses grow.
Their substance is not that of purple shadows
That stalk bare hills.
Someone carted resinous boards and shingles
Along that vague white road that mars the sage.
Someone built the house:
Fitted its beams and squared its window-frames . . .

The gaunt hills stood by silently,
The stark plains made no protest.
So silently they watched that in the end
The builder heard them speaking:
Heard them tell of loneliness and madness,
Of white stars that never care at all
For what man fashions . . .

The house has stood forsaken
For a long while now . . .

This Is the Hour . . .

This is the hour when the earth runs eastward in shadows:
Shadows of trees that are longer than ever a tree was tall;
Shadows of stubby fence posts that under the glare of the
　　noontime
Were stiff between plain and heaven, abashed and far too small
For the space they were set to frame. Now lithe and slender
　　they run.
Shadow-stencils of branching weeds: these would outdistance the
　　sun
That is level-shafted and golden; these would go free and wide.

This is the hour when the train runs eastward to darkness,
With the soundless prairie shadows running on either side.

Manhattan

Once, I laid fingers on a brittle pod
That dangled from a clump of jewel weed;
And at my touch, a sudden spurt of seed
Peppered the sod.

At five o'clock, the sun looks from the west,
Lingering on the level Palisade;
And its thin tapering finger-touch is laid
Upon this office-city.
                    Quickly pressed
Out of their pod-confinement, people scatter,
Tapping concrete with small staccato patter.

To a Man Who Believes a Loud Voice Proves More Than a Still Small Voice

Must you shout?
              If you are speaking truth,
the universe has subtle ears to hear.
If you are not . . .
              I still ask,
must you shout?

Tantrum

This day is a child that will weep
Till it fall asleep.
It tossed
The sun like a scarlet ball
And watched it fall . . .
Now it is lost
Behind a leaden, lumpy cloud-bank. Now
The day has puckered up an angry brow.
Round spattering tears are warm
Prelude to tantrum storm.
This day will weep
Till it fall asleep.

City River

These are the weary waters.
                              All their songs
Are hushed as are the beaten songs of men
Who have bowed too long, too long beneath a load
Ever to sing again.

Ripples curved to catch the glint of sun
Lie oversmeared with grimy streaks of oil;
And only one who had lived much with waters
Would hear the muffled chantey of their toil.

Hands Laid Upon the Wind

Hands laid upon the wind can only bless
Long restlessness.
They cannot bid wind stay.
And if we feel the ages like a wind,
We can but lay
Our hands upon them with a mute caress.
Over the tenuous rim of space they blow,
Whither we cannot know.
Our hands will not dissuade them: what wind lingers
Because it feels the touch of human fingers?

Our lifted hands confess
Not the wind's need, but our own need to give
Our tribute to the Law by which we live.
This our compact that the stars have sealed:
That to long winds of earth and time we yield
Ourselves, to keep their law inviolate;
And we walk garmented in modesty
In the old presence of the sky, the sea,
The full-plumped planet, and forbear to prate
About the scintillant honors that we earn
As short-lived men;
                            and as a rich return
Shall Matter rest itself upon our will,
Lending its prowess that we may fulfill
The sharp creative urgencies that burn
Our souls like tinder.
                            Deepest falsity
It is to think that we are driven to choose
Between submission and high right to use
The Law that uses us.

Splendidly free
Are we to make our compact with the powers
That blow like wind across our straitened hours.

Man bends his brain and heart to shape from these
Fruits of his ecstasies . . .
And then with quietness that understands
The way of wind, lifts up his roughened hands
To bless
Long restlessness.

Perhaps

How strangely, now, spring dusk and we are one.

When time has slid with a broad even flow
Beyond the margins of all worlds we know,
When all the aeons that we dream are done,
When space has dwindled to a thin blue shore
That feels the lapping of eternity,
We who have walked the long curved road of ages
May stand once more
Enfolded by a twilight harmony.
Shall I then turn to you, or you to me,
With eyes deep-shadowed by a memory:

"I am not sure . . . but was there not a night
Somewhere before when flowering trees were white
Against a dim upthrust of city towers?
Was there a haunted interval between
A strident day, a night of veiled alarms . . .
Some moment wrought of blue-white mystery
When earth took back a city to her arms?"

So we may send remembrance down a trail
Too long, too vague to trace.
It cannot lead us back to linger here
In this charmed place.
After a brief searching, doomed to fail,
We may forget . . .
Our puzzled eyes may slowly clear . . . and yet
If I remain as I, and you as you,
We may in that strange hour
Stand on wide space as on familiar ground
And catch some fragrance of a tree in flower.

The Knower

All things speak to the wind . . .

For it alone are the growing-songs of the wheat field,
And the sage autumn wisdom of the corn;
Pine trees know it for a wise listener;
To it, the spent summer grasses make confession of their wishes,
And lake waters of their longing;
Old, rheumatic houses stir themselves at its coming
To share a creaking record of long memories . . .

So the wind goes lonely with knowing . . .

Another Sun Has Set

Another sun has set.
                    And one more day
Of those allotted to our life and love
Has gone its hooded, solitary way,
Stepping with slow precision in the footprints
Of yesterday.
The west is healed now of the crimson scar
It bore for brief rejection of the dark.
And where it burned, a single cool-eyed star
Comes diffidently, with a white compassion
For men who are
Lonely without the sun. Grateful, we borrow
From its serenity a quietness
With which to speak about a world-old sorrow
That days must go . . . about a world-old waiting
For tomorrow.

Week-end Casualty

She left her sneakers standing by the bed
Where she had kicked them off after the game,
And had slipped on white sandals in their stead.
They do not know she will not come again.
They did not hear the crash, nor hear how pain
Wrenched from her in one cry her vibrant will.
It lies not in their province to explain
How at the heart of chaos she lay still.

On Determinism and Free Will in Human Affairs

There's no way out.
                    Figure it as we will,
We all must take the road to Kingdom Come.

But must we therefore choose to thumb a ride
On the band-wagon?

Ballad of the Star-Eater

I

Hunger assailed me
  With sharp cold pain.
I had searched for food,
  And searched in vain.

I had found no berries,
  No pulpy root;
And the boughs above me
  Bore no fruit.

So I lay in the grass
  And gnawed a blade,
And—I can't be sure—
  Perhaps I prayed.

I only know that
  Suddenly
A splendid knowledge
  Came to me:

Stars were twinkling
  Overhead—
On these I knew
  I might be fed.

So up I rose
  With quick, glad cry,
And began to scale
  The wall of the sky . . .

II

Here was a crevice,
  There a cleft—

So I went climbing,
   Right hand, then left.

My breath came short,
   The quick air stung,
But I *thought* brave songs
   As I climbed and clung.

Below, the horizon
   Stretched and grew
Till the earth swung free
   In a tide of blue.

Weary and stiff—
   But fiercely proud—
I swung at last
   To a ledge of cloud.

Then stars were around
   And over me—
Rare, ripe nuts
   On a heavenly tree.

I crushed and cracked them
   And crunched the meat.
Oh, they were rich
   And spicy sweet!

I crushed and cracked them,
   And from my hand
The shells slipped down
   In a meteor band . . .

III
When strength flowed through me
   From toe to crown,
I left my cloud-perch
   And came on down.

I can still see sky-dust
   On toe and heel
Where I dug for footing;
   And I still can feel

The curve of clouds
   Where I clung to these
With gripping fingers
   And gripping knees . . .

Now I walk the earth
   Without a care,
Though roots elude me
   And boughs are bare.

For stars still prickle
   My fingertips,
And the taste of stars
   Is warm on my lips.

I fear no hunger
   With sharp cold pain . . .
If it dare assail me,
   I will climb again.

Prayer for These Times: 1933

Now I lay me down to sleep . . .
Cool is the pillow beneath my head,
Crisp and cool the linen sheet,
Ample and soft the generous bed.

Nothing I lack that peace requires.
Surely will slumber be long and deep.
Yet—here I lie in the peopled dark,
Counting something . . . that is not sheep.

Counting the men who trudge the night
To beg a coin for a scanty supper
(Heavy the rhythm of broken shoes,
Flapping sole and wrinkled upper);

Counting the men with a bench for bed,
And a brittle wind for counterpane,
A ceiling above them of sullen cloud
Dragged low by a ponderous weight of rain;

Counting the women in narrow rooms
Who stare at darkness and wildly plan
How a meal for six can be made, tomorrow,
From what might nourish one slender man;

Counting the women who lie so still
The very bones of their bodies ache
Rather than let their anguished men
Know that they, too, are lying awake;

Counting the youths in whom despair
Like a quickened seed spreads root and stem:

Their flesh is taut with a pent-up power,
But the world has never a need of them.

I pray the Lord . . . but how shall I pray
That He shield my soul like a precious spark,
And cherish it well, while the eyes of woe
Stare at the unresponsive dark?

I pray . . . that so long as there yet remain
Hunger to feed and thirst to slake,
I may be saved from a suave content.
And this I ask for Jesus' sake.
                              . . . Amen

Anno Domini: 1934

At the time of year when sober dusk comes early,
We tramped together the long grey streets of our city,
And our steps were brisk with the need of warmth in our veins.
We saw how the city let the autumn leave it
Naked and sparse and cold as a winter wood.

Because the sun sank red in the shrouded west;
Because in the street the traffic lights flicked red,
We stopped to buy one scarlet flower for my coat,
And buried it deep in fur that cuddled my shoulders.
Wrapped in its fragrance we tramped through the deepening
    twilight.
Our joy was a scarlet flower, was a flame that leaps
In a room that holds no other light but a fire.
Scarlet flowers were our intimate words and our laughter . . .

Then from a doorway hunched a man, his voice
A whimper, an asking sob in the dimness . . .

You put a coin in his hand . . . and our joy went with it . . .
And slithered between his fingers and broke to bits:
To futile jagged bits on the ringing pavement . . .
And we had to leave it there when we walked away.

The Eye Sees . . .

By peering from her window
In a certain tip-toe way,
She could glimpse a meager strip of park
And, beyond, the bay
Where snub-nosed ferries pushed their awkward courses
Night and day.

And there were words that she had said so often
She thought them true:
"Of course, our rooms are dark and crowded,
And far from new . . .
Sometimes the stairs are long in climbing . . .
But there's the view."

Public Library, New York: 1934

This is the corner where pigeons circle,
Cleaving with their curved wings the stagnant air.
In grey-blue whirl, they lift and circle,
Circle and settle . . . and go nowhere.

This is the corner where lost men linger,
Hunching thin shoulders when north winds blow.
Here they huddle in an endless waiting . . .
Waiting for nothing . . . with no place to go.

Spoken and Unspoken: 1938

Thank you, porter . . .
                    (Yes, you can carry my bags.
They're heavy, as usual: as usual, loaded down
With a lot of things I probably won't need.)
Lower 3, Car 12 . . .
                    (Now, what can I carry for you?
The dark injustice that makes you the burden bearer
With never a question of what you might be instead?
All right . . . that's fair enough.
                        Here, help me a moment
To get that load settled squarely on my shoulders.)

Hand-Organ Song

The songs of men, the sorrow-haunted songs,
Have been old bearers of an older grief.
On them we lay the burden of our living . . .
And win relief.

But even song should not be made to bear
Such loneliness as this: the thinly sweet
Twirl of an organ where a broken man
Makes broken music in a twilight street.

Hospital

From blurred depths of anaesthetic stupor
Where consciousness drooped in a vague defeat,
I arose once more to light and meaning,
And friendly noises of a twilight street:
  A dog's gruff bark; the suck of vacuum tires;
  Rasp of a broom that swept dry leaves away;
  Slam of a door; a motor's quickening pulse;
  The swish and patter of a garden spray;
  Voices; tramping feet; and shifted gears;
  And rippled laughs of children at their play . . .
Deep was the vaporous peace of anaesthesia
Where neither pain nor fear could be discerned.
But Life called to me from a twilight street
. . . And I returned.

In a Japanese Garden

The goldfish leaps with a flash,
With an arrogant flip of a forked tail . . .
And is only a flit of color,
Gold through green,
  To be glimpsed . . .
  And forgotten . . .

The turtle paddles an awkward way
To the pond surface.
Lifts an absurd encumbering shell
And a foolish head with old vague eyes.
The turtle looks around with wistful expectancy . . .
  Is laughed at . . .
  And remembered . . .

Rejection of Romantic Melancholy

It does not seem, today, a noble thing,
Nor very brave,
To waste our span of living in long protest
Against the grave.
For all around, upon this pulsing earth,
Minds powered with flesh and bone
Are showing themselves dependably inept
At using years they own.
When we can say that no man willingly
Is author of man's grief,
With more conviction may we chide the Scheme
For making life too brief.

To One Who Thinks God Wears a Uniform

Let us trust in God—with moderation.
Of course, He will defend our nation
In time of war: He has inclined
Toward that end His mighty mind.
But let us not suppose that He
Could settle matters peacefully.

Question

Is any Power equipped to underwrite
The flimsy credit of this mutable world?

Above dark roofs go up the pillared white
Columns of smoke that softly are uncurled
Against blue dusk in thin diminishment
Until no smoke remains.
                              I strain my eyes
To read the invisible signature they scrawl
Upon the ample parchment of the skies.

But nothing there is written for my sight . . .
Unless in stars that fleck the ancient night.
Perhaps some promise that a God dictated
Is by star-points divinely punctuated.

Be Not Deceived

Be not deceived by any scarlet leaf,
By any twinkling yellow leaf that flies,
Into belief that every flaunting one
Gladly, blithely dies.

And if I spoke far otherwise than this
When autumn woods were close on every side,
Crying, "How gay it is!" that was the tribute
Pride pays to pride.

For you and I, and all things animate—
Each flower, each calling bird, each tree—
Must share with one another, while we live,
A brave conspiracy:

Knowing that life swings by a slender stem—
And knowing, besides, that it is very fair—
We must make gesture out of loneliness,
Betraying no care;

We must weave songs to fortress our frail days
And lift them boldly under the wide sky,
Chanting again—again—and yet again,
"We do not fear to die!"

What do we gain by all our proud deceiving? . . .
That, it may be, no man shall ever know.
Perhaps we shape our immortality
Beyond the flow

Of shifting, changeful matter . . .
                                    This is sure:
I would go outward like the flaring cry

Of scarlet leaf, of yellow twinkling leaf
On windy sky.

And woe to him who, on my day of going,
Pricks with a searching word my last defense.
And peace to him who cries, "How gay a thing!"
Sharing pretense.

All Praise To Man

Poor clumsy Nature, with what makeshift tricks
Does she accomplish death.
How oddly does she wait on accident,
On age, or on disease for checking breath.
With what embarrassment must she behold
The subtle versatility of man
Who, born to dread of dying, employs his art
To stretch the span
Of years allotted to his use; then bends
His carefully tended skill
To fashion instruments that can endow
His smallest finger with such power to kill,
Such power to heap the earth with broken dead,
That humbled Nature droops crestfallen head.

This Easter Day

Easter Day . . .
Speak of the Miracle: the Stone of Death
That Life has rolled away . . .
    Yet it is not enough that body rise
    Astonished and astonishing in newness.
    Man has said—and he will say again,
    And will be right in saying—the body grows
    Even as grass grows on a windy hill.
    And like the grass it withers.
                        And though flesh
    Should trick the grave that thought to hold it fast:
    Should rise and walk: it would but walk to find
    Another grave, some other time and place.
    If man is more than grass, the proof is elsewhere:
    Not in the muscled movements of the flesh.

    As each man asks of Life the kind of proof
    He thinks he can believe, so doubting Thomas
    Touched the puckered wound—and was convinced.
    It is a different evidence I seek.
    (This Easter Day too many young men die
    In blood atonement for our human folly:
    There are too many wounded hands and feet.)

This Easter Day,
Heavy, heavy are the Stones of Death
That Life must roll away.

    So in fair April weather I will go
    Looking for Him wherever I can find Him—
    And well we know the likely looking-places.

Where two or three together seek the truth,
There is He in their midst, a fellow-seeker.
He is the passer-by who stops to watch
Where little children play—and the smallest child,
Not quite knowing why, looks up at Him and smiles,
And does an extra skip and twirl of gladness.
He liked to eat with friends. I will do well
To look where friends sit down around a table
And are so lost in talk, in a few moments,
They half forget to eat.

                  I will remember
He liked an open hillside where He could
Get vista in His soul; or near at hand,
Could crush the ripened seed-pods of the grasses
With thinking fingers . . . and with thinking eyes
Could study in His palm the tiny seeds.
He was a man of healing: I will look
Where suffering flesh is quieted by fingers
Wise in the ways of flesh . . .

               And I will go
Where workmen—carpenters and fishermen—
Are at their daily jobs, for that would be
A likely place to find Him, and to hear
His words fall true as the curled shavings fall
From the planed board.

             And He will firmly be
God's Angry Man wherever persecution
Denies His law of life; that men are brothers.

So in fair April weather I will go
Looking for Him wherever I can find Him . . .
How shall I know if I stand in His presence?
In my own heart are heavy stones of darkness:
Stones of prudence and of apathy . . .
Stones of self-concern that shut away
From light and life the self that I might be.
Wherever these stones of death are made uneasy
In their deep sockets, and are rolled away,

There is the presence of the risen Lord . . .
There is the Resurrection and the Life . . .

Easter Day . . .
Speak of the Miracle: the Stones of Death
That Love can roll away . . .

Let There Be . . .

Let there be as much of shining light
Upon the landscape of the human mind
As on this slope and meadow in this hour.

Shadow, here, is but a strand of darkness
Woven through gold and various living green.
It is a movement; not a moveless weight
Stolid and heavy, but the earthward image
Of wings in flight, and clouds.
                                        Standing alone,
With this wide field around me, and in flower,
I feel the stubborn walls of selfhood crumble
Until I scarcely know dividing line
Between the psychic integer—myself—
And all I am and am not, and yet am;
And all I shall be, through swift hours and slow,
And dark and shining hours, until I die . . .
And all that others like myself, and different,
Will be when I am gone, until they die . . .
And on and on, running upon time's meadow
As wind runs here, and shadow of a wing . . .

John Doe, Jr.

Among the Missing . . .
               I think he always was—
Only no one thought to mention it before . . .

He was the boy who didn't make the team
although, God knows, he tried: his were the fingers,
always too eager, that always fumbled the ball.
He was the fellow
people forgot to invite when they planned a party.
After the party, once in a while, they would say,
"We should have invited John." But that was after;
and most of the time they did not think about it.
John thought about it: thought of the laughter and music.
He was the chap who dreamed that his loneliness
might somehow find in words a redemptive beauty:
the yearning youth who sent his poems and stories,
bundled in hope, to editors—and found them,
paired to rejection slips, in his mail-box, later.
He was the man, defeated by diffidence,
who waited in line—and who did not get the job . . .

Only war had use for him, and only
long enough to lose him . . .
                 Among the missing . . .

Are Not My Hands My Own?

Are not my hands my own?
                              How is it, then,
That I stand here alone within my kitchen,
Intent upon the making of a pie,
And suddenly my mother's hands have slipped
Inside of mine . . . and mine are only gloves
Made flexible by what she wills to do
With flour and salt and shortening?
                              I stare down:
My hands, proved mine by permanent signature.
And yet . . . their motions . . .
                              I have seen before
Fingers that held a pie-plate in mid-air
Upon their tips that spread to balance it;
And I have seen a hand that slid a blade
Around the pie-plate, neatly shearing off
Unwanted crust that dangled to the board
To crumple there into a little heap.
This is familiar. But it was not I
Who poised the plate or drew the cutting blade.
That was my mother . . .
                              And if this be I,
How do I know to the last small detail
The feeling that was intimately hers—
Just as she must have learned, upon some day
(And felt her fingers halt with quick surprise),
The sense of having other hands slip in
To use her hands, their muscles and their joints,
To work an older will with flour and salt.

This is the ancient comfort: the deep knowing,
In heart and bone and sinew, that I stand
Never alone so long as I can share—

Here in my kitchen, here in my little hour—
The modest drama of man's staying alive:
A quiet drama played in the small sounds
A spoon makes against a mixing bowl . . .
The little slap of dough upon a board:
Sounds all too slight to hear above the guns
That shrill the desperate drama of man's dying;
But sounds that will be there when the tired guns
Have grumbled into silence: always there . . .

So I stand here alone within my kitchen—
Flour on my hands, and centuries at my elbow—
As though I had come back to some beginning
To take another look at chart and compass.

Resistance Movement

When wind goes high in the night, shrilling its loneliness,
There are trees I am glad to remember.
Out where the cold grey curl of the surf
Climbs the Monterey coast,
Cypresses cling to the rocks.
What stooping before the wind
Those cypresses mean to do
Has all been done.

When fear sweeps over the world, shrill as a lonely wind,
Bleak as a wind in the night,
There are men I am glad to remember.

War Profiteers

While men grow florid in philanthropy
By offering up scant measure of the coin
Which first they studied shrewdly to purloin,
And which they will recover presently,
Why be surprised that when a limping peace
Returns a fragment of the youth war took,
These gentlemen who won a gold increase
Learn absentmindedly a modest look,
Or stand erect in patriotic pride,
Forgetful that it was not they who died?

If the Walls of This Room: 1942

If the walls of this room we have loved go down in rubble,
And all the things that are ours by reason of love
Our fingers have had for their texture, our eyes for color and
    form:
If these go down and my body be left alive—
Whole, or broken—I will longest remember
Evenings like this.
                   Of all the heart can know
Evenings like this are the furthest remove from war:
They are what peace is: they are what war has killed
In ten thousand thousand rooms around the world.

The tongues of men have squandered the name of peace
Where no peace is.
               They have spent the beautiful name
On the armed truce, on the circling of adversaries
That measure each other's strength . . . and wait to strike.
Because they have wasted this name they have never known
What dies in war.
             They have been naming as peace
What is almost war compared with evenings like this
In ten thousand thousand rooms where husband and wife
Love, and speak not of love, but of little things
Their love has chosen and cherished; where father and son
Talk of the tall son's work, and the father proud . . .

This is peace: the fact that I can look over
And see the two of you there, the lamplight shining
On your two dark heads, on your hands that carry within them
Gentleness man has learned from the touch of things
Loved by the hand and heart.
                 This only is peace . . .

If I walk to the window, stand with my back to the room,
Eyes close to the pane, hand shading the light,
Beyond my reflected image I can see
Our garden under the moon: the pools of shadow . . .
The ivory silence over the open lawn.
And it is peace. My eyes see only peace.
It is the heart that endures a further sight,
Knowing in pain that under this same full moon
The bombers fly . . . thanking the light of the moon
For the flawless gleam it lays on target-roofs . . .
For the shimmer it lays along a guiding river.

If the walls of this room we have loved go down in rubble,
And all the things that are ours by reason of love:
If these go down . . . and if my body goes down,
Broken as they by war, it will still be true:
Evenings like this are peace.
                              It will still be true.

Twentieth-Century Moon

Under the moon, the glazed white cities lie.
Across the moon, the dark-winged bombers fly.
Under the moon, the ruined cities die.

Moonlight belongs to lover and to fool.
Bow down the heart that moonlight can be cruel.

Throughout long ages, man, who feared the night,
Was grateful to the moon: when it shone bright,
His feet and heart went sure beneath its light.

Moonlight belongs to lover and to fool.
Bow down the heart: man has made moonlight cruel.

Grave Victory: Hiroshima

Let man, this day, look gravely on man's face,
Searching to read the future written there.

For it has come to pass: the miracle;
The tragedy; the terror—any name
That triumph, fear, or foresight may devise.
The hard fact holds: the basic atom-stuff
On which the structured universe stands firm
Has now been cloven by the brain of man.
With infinite precision, delicate touch,
Man has released on man intended death
Shaped from the power that holds the sun in place.

As echo answers echo, far and farther,
So from the spot where flesh and stone and steel
Lie fused in common chaos, there moves outward
Event beyond event in causal chain,
With no one knowing the end: the time or place
Where consequence may fade.
                      The columned smoke
That rises from the shaken, cratered earth
Is sculptured by the wind into a form
We squint our eyes and strain our hearts to name:
It may be Freedom . . . or it may be Death.
This smoke will drift and many winds will blow
Before our recognition of that form
Is clear and certain, stated in history.

Let man, this day, consider with grave mind
The bannered headline and the radio comment.

Subtract the featured fact of one bomb's falling,
And all the news is ordinary: labor
Protests delay in reconversion planning;

Stocks tremble at the word of rumored peace;
A university puts forth a plan
For liberal education; congressmen
Go on record, saying so and so . . .
Nothing is here we have not learned by heart.
Yet the mind, the soul, the conscience bodied forth
In this day's dole of happenings all seem changed:
For news now looms in startled silhouette
Against the flare of light where atoms perished
Like little universes going dark.

Let man, this day, look gravely on the face
That looks back from his mirror, eye to eye.

He makes more difference, now, this common man
Who is earth's Everyman.
                              For we have crossed
Some equinox of destiny. Together
We walk tall-statured toward the light of peace
Or slither back to the primordial slime.
It has come to pass. An item of daily news:
God's atom, now, weapons the fallible hand
Of men who yet see darkly.
                              Let us pray . . .

In Central Park: 1945

In Central Park
Children play at the blue-dusk hour
That is prelude to dark.
Their words ring clear as the lights that flash
Spark on spark.
Zippered up to a woolen semblance
Of tumbling cubs the small ones play,
Rolling and bouncing among the shrubs,
While from the west the twilight rubs
The stain of day.
On a slope too dim for proper sight
Lanky boys still pitch a ball,
And strike . . . and miss . . . and laugh and call,
Reluctant to admit the night.

We know the breeze that is fan to their faces,
And the sponge of earth that is cool to their feet.
In other years and other places
We have learned what makes a twilight sweet,
And what makes youngsters disallow
Each day's defeat.
As once we lingered, they linger now,
In hope that darkness will forget
The haste of its coming, and will come
Not yet . . . not yet . . .
Though one star pricks . . . and another pricks,
They linger still.
No use: for time is against their will—
Time no dallying can deceive.
Blue dusk yields to bluer night . . .
And in twos and threes the loiterers leave . . .

A brisk wind brushes over the grass
That lies rumpled and tramped by the feet that played.
Here and there, late walkers pass
Into lamplight and into shade.
Then there are only you and I
And the faint few stars of a city sky . . .
And our silent pledge that for children's sake
Must the world's peace be made.

Translation

Tawny wind-rippled sand dunes
Billow back from the shore line
Wave upon wave:
The alien speech of ocean translated
Into the language of earth.

Porthole

Through the porthole I can see
One tiny circle of blue, cloud-flecked . . .
Because it is there,
I know there is also
The infinite sky—remote, mysteriously sure.

Spring Rain

Only the leaves of the beech had words to say
About the soft rain.

The new grass,
The little flowers,
And I
Were grateful in silence.

Floating Things

I would borrow the reticent poise of floating things:
    Of the stem-tethered water lily
    That lifts a proud, clean chalice to the sun;
    Of the slim canoe that rides,
    Effortless,
    On a green depth of lake;
    Of the earth
       that holds the water lily,
       that holds canoe and green lake,
       that floats, proud and clean,
       through a blue silence,
       cutting a furrow of stars.

April Hour

Because of an hour we spent in an April wood,
　Where mosses cushioned the roots of trees
　And climbed the encircling stones,
I will trust Life—as I would trust
　A sun-warmed rock behind my shoulders;
I will handle Life gently—
　As I would press my fingertips upon moss.

To Be Sung Out of Doors Only

Gold is ready reward for those
Who take the path to the buttercup meadow
With sun so straight above their heads
That they cast no shadow.

Silver coin will be added, too,
If they outlinger the swift day's flight
And curve white palms to catch the glimmer
Of sleek moonlight.

Diamonds will slip with a crystal clink
Into the pool that is edged with clover . . .
Dipping fingers can scoop them out
When stars lean over.

Of Love and Laughter

I should have thought this world would be
Large enough for two;
But I had scarcely reckoned
On the size of you.
To be sure, I did notice
As we roved across the meadow
Early this morning,
That you cast a long shadow.
And when the red sun balanced
On a tight-rope western hill,
Your shadow was a mighty one:
Long enough to fill
The palm of the valley
That we had left behind.
But even now, in darkness,
Every cranny of my mind
Is so crowded with your presence
That, sun or no sun,
I acknowledge that my world
Is but large enough for one.

And that being the case,
It is well that we are one.

Sun

The ceremonious sun may rise and set
A thousand times, yet dodge the commonplace.
He knows the art of gesture.
                                    Up he comes
With amber clouds drawn close to frame his face.
Or he comes lagging wanly up a sky
Shrouded in grey. Deliberately he goes,
Monk-fashion, scholar-fashion. But a whim
Plays sudden havoc with his austere pose.
And we who have gone sobered to his mood
Are shocked to find him traipsing down the west
Wearing red shoes, a feather in his cap.
We blink our eyes, and hasten to divest
Ourselves of our own gloom. Ashamed to walk
Like trudging porters weighed by human ills,
We brighten up perceptibly. The sun
Dons leaf-brown fog . . . and sighs behind the hills . . .

We say man is capricious, and we hold
Crossed fingers as a symbol that is meet
In our appraisal of him. But the sun
Takes precedence for unabashed deceit.

On a July Afternoon, for Example

Sometimes Nature descends upon this City
As an indignant mother upon a grimy child:
Wind sweeps the dust away in swirling eddies;
Rain thuds down implacably,
Scrubbing reluctant wall and street
With a grim thoroughness,
Until the City, gasping for breath,
Stands forth in pristine freshness.
Then, with wrath expended,
Nature retires, righteously triumphant:
"*Now* will you keep clean!"

The City stands a moment,
Bewildered,
Staring upon this unexpected self;
And then, forgetful-eyed,
Resumes its interrupted joy
In making mud pies.

Now Morning Comes

Now morning comes upon me once again,
Bringing anew its clean gift of surprise
That stars can pale so soon in the white east,
That sun can be so gracious to the eyes
Of one who welcomed darkness as a friend
Some little hours ago.
                              Now light, unfurled,
Reaches before me like a sea whose shore
Is lost below the curved rim of the world.

Sun-gladdened, I arise—to poise, to spring
With swift white motion into gilded spray
That curls and blows along the lifted crest
Of the slow-flowing golden tides of day.

These are the sounding waters I must cleave,
Tasting their salty danger and delight,
Before I lean again on dusky shores
Made quiet by the benison of night.

Valentine

I do not know what use your heart can make
Of this small song I sing.
Out of my own need I have shaped the slight
Unnecessary thing.
Word follows careful word, and yet can say
Nothing new:
My eyes and hands a thousand times have said
The same to you.
You know, as you have known through all the years,
That in our love I live.
And yet in needless song I must repeat
My need to give.

Luna Moth

Before the moon had risen, moonlight came
On soft wings to our window: hovered there
Above the sill a moment, caught, and clung.
But even as we watched, the eastern sky
Took sudden whiteness from the coming moon . . .
And then the moon was there . . .
                              We raised our eyes:
"Thank you. We got your message."

Proud in Sunshine

This is the ledge where poison ivy clung
In ownership that I assailed of late.
Now a rock garden burgeons in the sun.
And I, in sun, can sit and contemplate.
Phlox, dwarf iris, and anemone
Of this dark feast of earth are bright partakers.
I tucked the roots of each into their place.
Now am I proud companion of all Makers.

Now, in this hour, I think I understand
Why God relaxed upon that Seventh Day
And praised the novel product of His hand.

Summers

Green New England hills
silvered by summer rain
laugh to one another
under a flecked sky . . .
And I remember,
across three thousand miles,
a land where brown hills hump themselves in the sun
and stretch out under the cobalt heavens
for a long siesta.

If the Touch Be Lacking . . .

Hungry for apples ready to our eye
But not our hand, we tried to shake them down.
They would not fall . . .
                    We gave them up as green.

But wind came casually across the orchard,
Saw them, and paused to give the fruitful tree
A proper shaking . . .
                    Apples tumbled down.

I've noticed this before: it's not enough
To have the hope or hunger: there must be
The magic touch to make the wish a fact.

Water Song

One does not weary of the voice of waters.

Springs gurgle from seeping banks;
Cataracts crash from rock to sounding rock;
Rain patters on windows, drips from the overhand of eaves;
Sea-breakers pound the long sand-beaches . . .

And there is no weariness in hearing them.

For in a fettered universe, the waters—
Earth-bound, rock-bound, moon-bound—
Sing themselves free.

Intention

If there be foothills in eternity,
If there be mountains, we will climb them,
Side by side on roads to the high pastures,
One after one on gritty trails to the peaks.

If none there be, our hunger will create them.
Memory will provide the needed substance.
The Wasach and Sierras and the Big Horns,
The Smokies and New England's spinal ridges:
Jumbled to fruitful chaos, these will rise
Responsive to love's edict, *Let there be . . .*
Let there be foothills,
Let there be mountains.

Angel Wings

One day a leaping goldfish
Glimpsed the crimson poise of a dragonfly.
And so faith grew
That over the surface of the mortal pond
Hung an infinite heaven of airy bliss
Where sainted goldfish drifted leisurely
On angel wings.

Caution

Upon my hand a single bulging drop
Has struck and spattered; and the swift clouds warn
That prudent feet would hurry from a spot
Where grasses slant, and yellow leaves are torn
By sudden gusts that swagger up the hill.

And now since I—in spite of self—was born
A cautious heir of a roof-building race,
I must not pause to welcome the dark storm
That soon would fling chill silver in my face.
I must find wings to grace my laggard heels,
And leave behind me this wind-harried place.

Yet . . . some few reckless forebears I can claim
Whom weather did not bid to go or stay.
Only the wonder of the world could tell them
When they should try for fleetness, when delay.
None but their laughing ghosts will ever know
If I race homeward by the longest way.

Summer Is Over

Summer is over. Oh, the leaves are green—
Green as they were before.
Yet swear I, by all Summers I have seen,
That this one now has yielded at its core.
Deliberate rain that blurs the rounded hills,
Steadily falling from an ashen sky,
Is other thing than the swift storm that fills
A summer hour with clamor and thuds by.
And yesterday I marked how wayside weeds
Were tawny on their stalks; and a bird's call
From grasses slanting heavy with their seeds
Was throaty warning of approaching Fall.
Summer is over now. I know . . . I know . . .
Though leafy with bravado it may stand,
Signs of remove are everywhere. Just so—
In just such little ways—from sobered land
I have seen Summer and Summer and Summer go.

Letter to My Mother

Here are pressed leaves that you may have for keeping.
I found them where the high trail climbs the hill.
There leaves lay deep in rusty brown and scarlet
To make a whispering carpet, and to fill
The hollows scooped by time in lichened stone.
I chose these two from all the rustling horde.
A tree has used them. They are yours to own.

The Ancient New

There is no thing more strange than a lone star
That pricks the darkening aftermath of sun:
No thing more strange than this . . . though the star's
                              coming
Was an old tale when man's tale was begun.

There is no song more lifted by surprise
Than a bird's song that cleaves the morning air
With certain ecstasy: no song more fresh . . .
Though all our fathers thus have known it fair.

There is no urge that carries more of wonder
Than the urge that draws green buds from winter trees.
There is no death more strange than a leaf's falling.
Earth's oldest patterns are renewed in these.

Lullaby

Earth has forgotten, now, all that the sun said,
Striding out boldly across the blue day.
Blithe though its words they have dwindled to silence.
Earth now listens to what the stars say.

What the stars whisper is all about sleeping:
All about poppies folded for repose;
All about bird heads tucked under bird wings;
And dreams that walk silently after eyes close.

Grand Canyon

Too far down the trail for surface sounds to reach
And too far up to hear the river's tumult,
We stood transfixed by silence:
Silence so absolute in authority
That we ourselves obeyed it. Where we stood
Voice had no place.
                           It was as though,
Spell-bound, we had been carried back through time
To a point before life's advent—when this earth
Was yet to learn the multiplicity
Of sounds through which the living say, "I'm here."

Then a bird called . . .
We dared to speak once more.

From the Pacific Palisades

Song is man's brave inadequate answer
    To questions traced on long sand beaches in phrases of foam—
    To questions scrawled by driven clouds on dark skies—
    To questions framed in the code of blinking stars.

Leafy Code

What this year can say in a leafy code
Has all been said:
There were cool green words; and, later,
Swift yellow words, and red;
And brown remarks that fallen leaves
Murmured under their breath:
Something about the clamor of crows,
The stillness of death.

Now earth rings brittle under heel;
Boughs rattle overhead.
What this year can say in a leafy code
Has all been said.

So the Good Die Young

She never said anything to make us stare.
But she lived her life with a certain air
Of knowing what the sun intends to do
With curly clouds, and why the blue
Of the ancient sky is always new.
She listened to people—and their words grew wise
Because of the wisdom within her eyes.
Lightly as leaves cling, the quick years clung
About her shoulders till her songs were sung.
Then she, at ninety, being good, died young.

Hate-Monger

His mind and double chin are of one stuff:
A quivering sauce-and-gravy supplement
To protoplasm that is his by birth.
Amphibian words forsake this primal ooze;
Slither and crawl; increase their confidence;
And soar on wings of rhetoric to reach
The lowest level of man's intellect.

Deep Fingers

This oak that shouts and tussles with the storm,
Fearless in laughter, stands against the shock
Not only with stout trunk and knobby limb:
Below, deep roots are intimate with rock.

Since first the polished acorn, lulled in loam,
Was stabbed by the brisk urgency of birth,
No branch has tried the alien paths of air
But knew a sister-branch embracing earth;

No leaf has held the amber weight of sun
Or tugged in summer wind but silently
Some root has crooked a finger into soil,
Intent to foster a long constancy.

And if, storm-dazzled, I bear gratitude
For this brave stoop of limb, this weathered bark,
My trust flows down to that inverted oak
That weaves a quiet staunchness in the dark.

A Slight Misunderstanding

The scholar, addressing his peers, employed the Greek:
"God is *agape*."
Next morning, a man, riding the bus to work,
Absorbed his daily quota of headlined news
Of crime and corruption, hunger and murder and fraud.
By happenstance, then, he came on the scholar's words:
"God is agape? Well, he has good reason to be."

Into Metaphysics

A swimmer who dives outward from grey rock,
Cleaving the water cleanly to its base
(That chilly green, that shadow-haunted place)
Returns with trophies of the silver shock:
On shoulder and lean thigh, a trembling flock
Of jewel drops that scatter at his pace
So that he treads on irridescent lace . . .
Across his lifted brow, a streaming lock.

So have I plunged me with a sharp-caught breath
Into that deep, that mystery-checkered pool
Of what man knows about this side of death . . .
Of what he dreams about the endless cool
Remote that lies beyond it. And I bear
The rainbow drops upon my hands, my hair.

New England Farmer

We who have learned to know him soon forget
The faint surprise
With which, as strangers, we saw blue and grey
Contend for mastery of his quiet eyes.
Such is the fitness of their rivalry
That wonder dies.

For we have seen him, many a sun-drenched day,
Serenely stand
To try the long horizon with his sight,
And the curved sky; and then, crowbar in hand,
Stoop down to wrest a grey and stubborn rock
From its deep socket in unfruitful land.

With Plato

So hushed a day is this that one sere leaf,
Floating earthward with compliant sigh,
Would send the echo of its whispering
Across the purple arches of the sky.
Along the hills, the russet hours go by,
Weaving no motion in the withered grass,
Shaking no bough of oak or sycamore
To mark the soundless trail by which they pass.

Oh such a day as this, the protean world
Feels the calm fingers of Eternity:
Each flaming bush now shadows forth the Bush;
Each tree assumes the image of the Tree
That feels no quiver of earth's transiency;
Each lake is but a copy of the long
Unfettered Water that no shore confines . . .
And silence but the reticence of Song.

We Do Not Know

We do not know whether our blessing reached them.
We spoke it, driving past, upon the family
That lived in the first house to show a light
Beside the long Canadian road we traveled
In the great dark that comes before the dawn:
One light upstairs; one in the kitchen ell.
"Cherish them, God, this day. Give them your peace."
We do not know whether a woman's hands—
Building the fire, setting the breakfast table—
Moved easier for our words; or a man's step
Grew sprightlier on the stairs . . .
We do not know . . .

For Keeping

Lifting spadefuls of earth and turning them down
To crumple beneath their weight the weeds they had bred;
Cutting and raking the dark-packed clods of earth,
On a late fall afternoon we made a bed
For the winter-sleeping bulbs of hyacinths.
Overhead
Birds were blown across the sober sky
Like showers of leaves. Around our feet and shoulders
Leaves were blown by.

Now in the winter frost has taken the earth,
Nipping it deep,
Ridging the surface, hardening the bed
Where hyacinths sleep.
The birds have gone, and the leaves forget to blow . . .
But the feel of the bulbs in our hands and the smell of the earth
We shall keep.

An Annual Affair

This is the time when crickets come indoors
To pay for warmth with singing.
                              It's no use
To try to keep them out. They will get in.
Nor is there valid reason to exclude them.
Mankind and cricketkind, upon this earth,
Have long shared knowledge that the place to be
When days shorten and the nights grow long,
Is where a fire is . . .
                    Crickets come indoors
For the same reason that a man comes in,
Stomping his feet and rubbing his chill hands:
Because they hear what weather has to tell them,
And know the hearthside as the place to be.

Prayer

Great God, I pray you, bring to birth this song—
This heavy song that lives and moves in me.
Let me bear fruit of this sharp pregnancy
With which I have been weighted over-long.
Each moment, now, I feel the twisted prong
Of pain that soars to quivering agony . . .
Yet am I blessed with this fertility.
I do not plead for ease . . . I shall be strong . . .

Lord, I have mated with your universe.
Loving so much its wind. its rainy mirth,
Its sudden slanting blue, its tranquil earth,
I yielded self—for better or for worse.
Anguish and glory now to me belong.
Oh, let me mother forth a swift, proud song!

With Honor

What the Professor knew about the stars
Had formed a bony structure for his thinking
And given to his mind an easy stride
Like that of his long body—as if he knew
The universe had room for any thought
That he was like to have. And in his talk
Orion entered, and the Pleiades,
With quite the intimate casualness reserved
By most of us for speaking of our friends.
We students in his classes could forget
That he was trying to teach us—if he was.
Rather, he seemed to find that universes
Were not uninteresting to think about:
All of them, or any part of them,
From a ten-foot-square back yard to Betelgeuse.
And there was something in the wordless way
He laid his hand upon a telescope.

Count Ten

(Count ten before speaking in anger.)

What shall we count to cool our angry pride?
Ten brittle digits standing in a line?
Oh, wiser far to count ten circling stars
That lean upon blue space: they will decline
To lend themselves to bitterness or pain.
Or we might count ten muted leaves that fall
Bearing a freight of sober autumn rain:
Ten leaves that fall, one here, one distantly,
In leisurely submission to the ground.
Or ten flecked pebbles lying in a pool
So hushed by dawn that the air holds no sound
Of water-motion. Or count ten mortal men
Who have come forth by the red gate of birth
To meet the wind . . . to learn the tang of laughter . . .
To wonder . . . and return into the earth.

For having counted, slowly we can lift
Our eyes to look on him who has offended,
Saying, "How large and strange this life we live . . .
Was I enraged with you? . . . Well, that is ended . . ."

As Ever

The old, old magic of the moon tonight
Has cast its phantom spell upon the sea:
Tides that mount in darkness fall away
In silver symphony.
And I, so newly come to a worn planet,
Am weighted with an ancient mystery.

Unlost

Candle flame buffeted by darkness,
Slow curve of purple iris petal,
Rainbow arch above a waterfall . . .
These I have seen—and these have passed away.
Have passed . . . whither?
Into the Great Nothing?

Then fearless shall I face the baffling Void.
For how shall Nothing take unto itself
All lovely things,
All fragile things that fade,
And not itself become
Majestic,
Clothed in wonder?

Big Dipper

Seven stars among a myriad—
Seven whirling furies of fire
Far set in space,
Held apart by baffling distances—
Strangers to one another.

. . . We glance up,
Conceive a shape,
And give a name.

On Watching Autumn Leaves Fly Upward

The poplar leaves twirl upward with a flourish,
Gold against blue—as though the sky could nourish
A blither sort of life than can a tree
That is committed to earth-dignity;
As though they had grown yellow with sheer yearning
To spurn the twigs they now are deftly spurning.

It is a good way to dismiss a year:
This twinkle of pure yellow on the clear
Large blueness of November. Better flying,
Though it be brief, than staid unjaunty dying.
The earth can wait until they want to rest—
And they will sleep the better for their jest.

Story

This is the story told by the tall brothers
Who used to come down from the hills in the fall of the year
To walk the streets of our town with their long stride.
They said that once they had seen, standing in moonlight—
And had seen only once—the woman of beauty
Who is the woman alive in all men's hearts.
Where a moonlit clearing opened among the balsams
They saw her standing . . . and knew they could love no other.
By the food they put in their packs for the long winter
They swore that their words were true.
                                    Some said they were lying.
Others said they were crazy. I didn't say either,
For I was a child, and their way of truth was my way.

And there was one twilight hour when I stood alone
Beyond our farm and before the rise of the hills,
Watching a white moth fly and a white moon rise,
And, on a sudden, knew I was not alone.
I turned and saw that the quiet two tall brothers
Had come beside me there, packs on their shoulders,
Crossing the meadow toward their homeward trail.
They stood in silence beside me and watched as I watched
The frail moth hovering white above white flowers.
Then one of them said, "We think you believe our story."
I looked at him: "You know I have never doubted."
His lean hands touched my shoulder, lighter than words,
As he smiled and said, "Then you will never be lonely."
And the other said, "Or else you will always be lonely . . .
But will never begrudge the price that has to be paid
For seeing the invisible beauty."

                                    They left me there.
I never saw them again. Years followed years . . .

And trails of my own choosing have taken me far . . .
I am older now.
                I am old enough to know
What I knew as a child: that only the speaking of truth
Can make men walk the earth with so easy a stride.
But I do not know—I never have come to know—
Which brother spoke truth to me about loneliness.

November Loss

The weight of rain upon each maple bough
Has brought to earth a sudden shower of leaves
That else had lingered through a tenuous day
To savor final draughts of autumn sun.
Naked branches, now,
Write intricate silence on a dripping sky.

And nothing can be done.
Not you—not I—
Not the inventive universe itself
Can lift one leaf to its forsaken place
Nor waken it to living melodies.

Only the trees,
Undoubting—undismayed—
Ponder within their bark-walled solitude
How they will shape, all in good space,
New leafy certainties.

An Old Farmer Dies

The Something that began eighty years ago
Is over now.
Who would suppose such quietude could come
To hands gnarled by the plow;
To feet so long concerned with heavy going
On clod and clover?
But the Something that began eighty years ago
Is over.

We are the neighbors who have heard his stories;
His talk of apples, horses, hogs, and grain;
His patient words about untimely frost
And lack of rain.
We knew him years and years . . . and only now
We know we cannot know
What ended here . . .
Or what it was began
Eighty years ago.

Always Near

Always I shall have stars to hold.

Beloved fields have now withdrawn in space.
I watched them dwindle; watched new lands unfold
Before my face.
The train has whistled to the mountain range,
Inviting peaks to echo shrill refrain.
Weary of mountains, it has made exchange
For slopeless plain.

But night comes down—and with it, every star
That in familiar heavens I called dear.
Stars are not left behind: so high, so far,
They swing in space that they are always near.

Dark Victory

The long doors of the dark have closed on me.
Although I batter till my knuckles bleed,
I cannot summon the light-footed dawn
To lift relentless bars; I cannot speed
The sun . . .
           Yet I can stand
In the proud halls of night without a dread.
I can withhold my futile, beating hand,
And lift my sight to cool stars overhead.
I can grow wise in silence and in space—
So when the dawn comes by to set me free,
I may walk out to meet the radiant day
Companioned by a dark serenity.

New Year's Eve

This day is soundless only if we count
As void of sound the crinkled leaves that fall,
Snipped by the cold, from hickory and beech;
Only if we ignore the flicker's call
And hammer-tappings, and the bluejay's screech.
This day is soundless only if we stand
Unmoving where we are: one step would break
The silence with the readjusting stir
Of bothered leaves; a dozen steps would wake
The snapping of stiff twigs, the sudden whirr
Of thicket-tracing wings.
                              Ourselves may go
Subdued by autumn hush; but all around,
In the old way that years have gone before,
This year is going in multiple small sound.

Winter Twilight

Call down the snow. Bid it fall soundlessly
Upon these streets that clamor their unrest.
Plead for the gift of its white excellence
To mask this town—which is ourselves, confessed
In a bleak outwardness of steel and stone
That carve their jagged lines across grey cloud.
Persuade the snow to visit these lean trees
And rattling shrubs, till every twig is bowed
Under a weight of gracious magic . . .
                                        Then,
Into the glimmering twilight, we will go
On strange hushed feet . . .
                        We will speak quietly
Of cities that man's dreaming might bestow
Upon a grateful earth—of clean white spires
Soaring and radiant as our brave desires.

Return

We hardly knew the road with the trees taller
By twenty years of growing; and four new houses
Where our eyes had thought to see an open field;
And clearings where there had been only thicket;
And branches where there had been open sky.
Almost, we stopped and turned: "This can't be right."
But then the curve . . . and the grey rock and the sumach . . .
And suddenly, the house . . .

                        And twenty years
Retreated soundlessly: went on tiptoe
To leave the spell unbroken . . .

                            Once again
We walked the flagstone path we had laid down,
And came to the door we had been first to open
And saw it was the same, with the same knob
Our tentative hands had turned on that first day
When we had ventured in, and within new rooms
Had stood upon new floors and felt around us
The reassuring mystery that is mark
Of all new homes—and knew it had happened again:
Again, the universe had countenanced
A comforting division of its size;
Again, the out-of-doors had let itself
Be clipped to window-images, to framed
Pictures of windy beeches in the sun.

It was all the same . . . and different . . .
                    And we stood
With hand on knob we did not try to turn,
Nor want to turn.
                    We had come back to see
That all was well: and all was very well . . .

We would not need to come this way again.

Make Room Among the Heroes

There is no form that walks upon this earth
More clad in impotence, more starkly grand
In fronting sharp betrayal, than the farmer
When one mad quirk of weather wastes his land.

"Not rain tonight . . . Oh, God, not rain tonight!"
Only his silence speaks the pleading word.
With sudden spattering drops the cold dusk falls . . .
The sun sinks luridly . . . the hills lie blurred

Beneath grey slant of storm. He lies awake
Through such long nights, and hears relentless rain
Mark off the trudging hours of his defeat
With gusty swishes on the windowpane.

He lies awake in loneliness and terror.
Tortured by a poignant power to shape
An image of a soggy morning world:
Of peaches split, of mildew on the grape.

And night when frost comes gliding out of season
With a deceptive beauty that can loot
In one crisp hour the treasure of spring blossom . . .
And petals darken unfulfilled in fruit.

And nights of anguish when stampeding wind
Wrenches an orchard heavy with its crop
Of half-ripe prunes . . . he lies awake to hear
The bleak staccato of the lost fruit's drop.

Never believe that man has tamed the earth,
Or that the years are harnessed to his need:
The rain, the frost, the wind confound his dreams;
And stubborn drought withers the stoutest seed.

But never think that earth has conquered man:
In heavy-footed majesty he plods
Across his wasted acres, and his eyes
Hold patience that would shame the patient gods.

He stands alone to front the universe
With Phoenix hope sprung from the ash of fear . . .
And when he speaks, the words fall somberly,
But punctuated by a phrase, "next year . . ."

Trinity

Fire is warm, and hope is warm, and love is warm—
These three
Stand firm against the encroaching cold:
A holy trinity.

Fire is mine, and hope is mine,
And love stands always near.
Yet strange, bleak winds around our walls
Are whistling fear.

They are the winds of knowing too well
How many homeless men
Will own not fire, nor hope, nor love
Again.

Talisman

The pebble in my pocket could not solve
The problem in my mind—although my fingers
Sought it as though their rubbing could elicit
An answer from its smoothness.
                              What it gave
Was not an answer, but a memory:
A memory of an autumn afternoon
When we two walked sandy and pebbly stretches
Along the northern shoreline of Lake Erie,
Leaning against the wind. And though the wind
Caught at our words and tossed them where it would,
We talked, exploringly, of old and new
Aspects of man's predicament on earth.

From all the thoughts we shaped that afternoon
One suddenly came forward to illumine
My present problem.
                    We can not ordain
The way a talisman will work its magic.

November

Cold wind shakes the furred heads of asters,
The faded goldenrod, the hairy woodbine.
No color there for any wind to find:
All are seed-dun.
Upon the hardened roadway where we tramp,
Collars turned up and hands thrust deep in pockets,
One stiffened oak leaf walks on starfish points.
We speak . . . and on thin air
Our breath becomes the pale ghost of a season:
"Snow before nightfall . . ."

Winter Again

Wind-beaten wings are dark on somber skies.
Lean trees whimper as they shake scant leaves.
And suddenly fear whines around my heart . . .
Winter again.

Why should I shiver at the thought of ice,
And long darkness,
And the shrill trumpets of the charging gale?
My walls are sturdy walls:
Though wind buffets them,
And drifts pile high to peer through every window,
These walls will stand
Encircling a warm security.

But no one is himself alone . . .
In me, the presence dwells
Of all who have known Cold as an ancient god:
Explorers of bleak lands where warmth became a tale of old
    romance;
Red men in forest lanes,
Watching leaves fall and wild geese fly,
And brooding on a season of thin living;
Prairie pioneers locked in white isolation;
These, and homeless men who wander an aimless way through
                        city streets
With their backs to the wind . . .
These have shivered when wings were beaten down a desolate
    sky,
When scant leaves rattled on lean trees.

And I am one with them.
Alone . . .

Suddenly small beyond self-knowing . . .
I face an old fear.
Winter again.

To a Skeptical Friend

You find it quaint that I can still employ
The name of God with reverent intent;
And I am happily disposed to grant
The honest justice of your wonderment.
For having heard the quibbling talk of men,
I should be much to blame could I not see
That my reliance on this ancient term
Must bear some fruit of ambiguity.
Knowing this, I may be ill-equipped
To marshall arguments to the defense
Of what, with gentle tolerance, you define
As my naive, inveterate innocence.
Yet this I offer: vainly I have tried
By logical device to thwart the claim
Of something potent in the universe
That still persists and still demands a name.
Perhaps the name of God is shabby now.
Would you prefer the One, the Over-Soul?
I only know that, living, I have need
Of way to designate the Subtle Whole.
Atoms are real; quanta are real enough.
Yet these are terms that still leave undefined
The power that could elicit from raw substance
Deft interplay of body and of mind;
That could determine how the stars would swing
In cosmical design upon blue space;
Or how an eagle's wing, remote and sure,
Can bring strange longing to a human face.
Some power beyond the known yet makes us seek
A fitting term for our acknowledgement
That we are ignorant of what occurred
To cause a universe.
                    I name it God . . .
If you protest, grant me a truer Word.

Question for City Hall

Who is traffic officer to the winds?
Who blows a shrill whistle
When a southeaster carrying bundles of dust
Collides at a sharp corner
With a racing southwester, leaf-laden?
Who takes charge when the two crash—
When dust and leaves fly in a swirl
And settle to the pavement
In surprised confusion?

December Moon

Do not speak. This crystal world would splinter
To iridescent fragments. We would spin
Dizzily into emptiness. White winter
Has made the air too frangible, too thin
To bear the weight of words.
                              Step cautiously
Along the stiffened ridges of the lane.
They yield with frosty crunching: it may be
The brittle earth cannot support the pain
Of our brusque feet. For see how one sharp heel
Pressed on an icy puddle can devise
Intricate sudden tracery, and reveal
Our too precarious footing.
                              Far more wise
To stand in voiceless fixity and gaze
Upon these strangely unfamiliar fields
Where frost and moonlight weave a silver glaze.
The trees and we shall print our inky shapes
On alabaster: trees as dark as death,
And all as rigid; we ourselves shown living
Only by lingering frosty whiffs of breath.

Now there is stillness. Not the flinty stars,
Not the globed moon, can wring the slightest sound
Out of the chilly heavens. No stir mars
The answering silence of the hardened ground . . .

Earth and we must alter. But tonight
Let us stand long, with eyes wide to remember
How changeless is a planet glimmering white
With the enchanted moon-spell of December

In Front of the Fire

Only beings half earth would dare to tame,
With axe and saw, wild apple trees and turn them
Into flame.
But only beings half god would let their plunder,
Falling to ashes, plunge them deep in wonder.

Agnostic, After a Fashion

These many months, now, have I carried with me
My credences—a somewhat random lot
Gathered from here and there, and borne along
Like rattling walnuts clutched in a paper sack.
One after one have I been drawing them out
And hefting each as one might heft a nut
To make surmise about the meat within.
Some were so light I had but little need
To crack their shells for added confirmation
Of their containing only wrinkled dryness;
And some held only a dust that worms had left
When they had finished with their noiseless nibbling;
But others were full weight, and crushing these
I found a fragrant meaty sustenance.

Like walnuts in a paper sack . . . and now
The last has met its estimate . . . the last
Has left its shelly fragments where I tossed them.
Now in my hand remains a wrinkled sack—
Something to lift to lips with final gesture,
To puff with air and slap to small explosion.
No other use.
                    Except that I remember
That in this season of the yellow harvest
New nuts are ripening that will rattle down,
Bouncing free from their frayed acrid hulls.
And if I chanced to come upon a tree
Where I could shuffle searchingly through leaves,
I might replenish my exhausted store
With full unblighted nuts.
                            In any case,
It does no harm to smooth and fold the sack
And carry it along.

Assurance

These stars will wait until we come again.
We need not fear. Their steadfastness is proof
Against the vagrancy of altered mood
That sends us homeward now, to seek a roof
Where fire awaits our coming.
                              In its glow
I shall scrawl out a letter to a friend;
Your turning pages will count off the hours
That have no other voice . . .
                              And then, day's end:
I shall put by my pen, and you your book;
We shall bank up the coals, and climb the stairs,
Content to leave to the soft-fingered dark
Our shadowy-cornered room, our empty chairs.

Tomorrow, we shall think and speak our thoughts . . .
We shall touch hands . . . and do each little chore:
The cooking of our food . . . our garden's care . . .
The brushing by of leaves before the door.
We shall make laughter out of bafflement;
And meet the wind . . . and watch the day's declining . . .

Then we shall stand again beneath these stars,
To feel how certain is their nightly shining.

Wild Asters

All who love New England love wild asters.
To love them not would be a heresy
Against the faith that Winter is a time,
And not forever.

Asters are the smoke of each year's burning.
Give them your love before the embers fall.

No Room at the Inn

And she brought forth her firstborn son, and
wrapped him in swaddling clothes, and laid him
in a manger; because there was no room for
them at the inn.—Luke 2:7

There is never room at the inn . . .
                                    There is never room
In the warm, well-lighted hostel for those who come
Poor, unrecommended, without connections
Seeking a place to bring a new dream to birth.

The night clerk is overbusy.
                              Important guests
Are demanding all the attention that he can give.
He would turn the strangers away with curt refusal
And put an end to the matter: "We're all filled up."
But there's likely to be somebody standing around—
The assistant manager, maybe, or a bellhop—
Who overhears and is troubled . . .
                              It's bleak outdoors . . .
And late . . . and these people are driven . . .
                              And besides,
There's something about them . . .
                              He doesn't know what, exactly . . .
But he wouldn't feel easy himself about turning them out.
He speaks in an undertone . . . and the bustling clerk
Lends grudging, impatient ear, and says to the strangers,
"There's a shed out back. You might find it better than
  nothing . . ."

There is never room at the inn . . .
                              And the dream is born
In the windy stable, making its own warmth;
Making its own clear light, and borrowing comfort

From the simple placid beasts, and the stablehand
Who comes and stands in the doorway, fidgeting
With his wish to help . . . and who digs up an extra blanket
And does not say that it comes from his own bed.

The dream is born without a headline report.
For a day or two there is talk where housewives meet:
"My husband says it's risky letting them stay there . . .
People like that . . .
                    It wouldn't surprise me any
To learn some things are missing after they leave."
"My brother stopped to talk with the stablehand.
He says that they're all right—decent and quiet . . ."
"Well, there's something *queer* about them . . .
                                        I always say . . ."
There are those who maneuver errands to take them close
To the open door of the stable.
                              And there are those
Who manage, when no one is looking, to carry over
A kettle of steaming soup and a spare shawl . . .

In the world as the world is, the dream starts growing.
But then there comes the day of astonishment:
Strangers rich in wisdom and this world's goods
Appear in town . . .
                    Eyes stare . . . and rumors fly . . .
Then it comes out: they are famous, important men
From somewhere off on the other side of the world.
And they've come all the way to visit those folks in the stable.
Very first thing, they asked where they could be found;
And went down there . . . went right into the place;
And a man who was watching says that they took out gifts—
Expensive, beautiful gifts—that would make your eyes
Pop right out of your head.
                          They talked a while . . .
Then disappeared as suddenly as they came . . .
"Something peculiar's going on . . .
                              Those people down there . . .
Maybe they're someone important, here in disguise."

"*I* say they ought to be watched . . .
                              Those men who came . . .
They were *foreigners*, weren't they?"
                              The manager of the inn
Hears the rumors, and has no way to decide
Which are true: if these are *important* people,
They should be in his best room, not there out back.
He knows how to handle guests: could even arrange
A special event in their honor . . .
                              On the other hand,
If they're trouble-makers of some sort . . .
                              Either way,
He stands to be made a fool; and the local wise men
Who ought to be able to help him are dunderheads:
They fumble and mumble, "Well . . ."
                              So the manager
Decides to go and take a look for himself:
Go and talk to the strangers: put it up to them
That his inn has a solid, respectable reputation:
That he can't afford to have anyone staying around
Who's out of the ordinary run . . . who starts people talking.

Then word is brought:
                    The strangers have gone in the night:
They have simply vanished.
                              They didn't take anything;
But it's queer they'd want to go slipping away like that,
Not telling a soul about it . . .
                              The stablehand
Picks up the folded blanket they left behind,
And smooths it with lonely fingers . . .
                              He's going to miss them . . .

There is never room at the inn . . .
                              And the kind stable
Is but a starting place for the growing dream.

Year's End

Winter has polished up the stars tonight
Until their points are thistle-sharp. Our fingers
Would be too wise to touch them. But our sight
Is an imprudent venturer: it lingers
Deliberate in its will to feel the bright
Stilleto barbs that heaven hones tonight.

Winter has buried under markless snow
The rocks, the roads, the tangled clumps of weeds.
Lacking these landmarks, hesitant feet forego
Accustomed ways. But thoughts have other needs:
They have a use for loneliness, and know
How to employ the vacancy of snow.

Ghost Day

Today has passed me by—
A slim grey ghost.

At first, I did not know . . .
It seemed but one of many days
That come and go.
But then a flickering shadow of bare boughs . . .
A certain wind that blew
Curled leaves in whispering eddies at my feet . . .
And all at once, I knew:

This was a phantom-day—
A slim grey ghost
Of one still autumn day I spent with you.

613 Royal

In the night—
   A fountain rising in silver shimmer,
   falling in silver sound;
   a white moth drifting
   from flower to white flower;
   black shadows of palms
   stenciled on moonlit walls,
   on moonlit flagstone walks . . .
And you said,
   "We shall not forget."

Days have slid into years, years into decades,
   since we lingered there, talking across a table.
   Death has silenced your voice.
   Fire, they say, has leveled that place we loved.
But I send my assurance out to find you:
   "I have not forgotten."

Brief Elegy

Never more . . . never at all
Will you speak of the roses over our wall . . .
Or your palm intercept a petal's fall.
Wind that swirls red petals down,
Oh, wind blow lonely.

Never more . . . never at all
Will you measure how young trees grow tall . . .
Will your throat echo the far quail's call . . .
Now in the dawn the whistling quail
Call for me only.

Forever

I think the friendly hills we loved so dearly,
You and I,
Will miss us as the streaming color fades
From sunset sky.
The trees will bend above our little path
And whisper low
Of all the quiet loveliness and peace
We used to know.
And they will dream that we are lonely too,
Since paths must sever.
They cannot know that you walk by my side,
Forever, ever.

Index of Titles

Index of First Lines